better together*

* This book is best read together, grownup and kid.

 akidsco.com

a
kids
book
about

a kids book about

ANGER

by Fabian Ramirez

a
kids
book
about

Printed in the United States of America.

A Kids Book About books are available online: *akidsco.com*

To share your stories, ask questions, or inquire about bulk purchases (schools, libraries, and nonprofits), please use the following email address: *hello@akidsco.com*

ISBN: 978-1-953955-52-4

Designed by Rick DeLucco
Edited by Denise Morales Soto

Interested in inviting Fabian Ramirez to speak at your school? Visit TopYouthSpeakers.com

Eden and Ava, be patient
with yourselves and others.

Intro

Fact: You will feel anger. No matter your age, something will happen that's out of your control, and the situation will make you angry. Don't be afraid to feel this strong emotion—feel it! Maybe you grew up being told to suppress your anger—don't! Maybe you've witnessed someone get angry—me too! Because it's natural. Humans were made to feel all kinds of emotions, and anger is no exception to that.

History is full of amazing people who managed their anger and brought about healthy change.

Want to learn how anger can encourage your emotional health? This book will help you understand how such a strong emotion, when recognized and managed, can be the motivator a person needs to bring about positive change.

Have you ever heard the song
"If You're Happy and You Know It"?*

*If not, check it out!

I love that song because it's about feeling happy!

Everyone loves
feeling happy, right?

But guess what?

We all feel moments of anger too.

I bet you've never sung
about anger though.

Let's give it a try.

"IF YOU'RE ANGRY AND YOU KNOW IT MAKE A FIST,

GRIND YOUR TEETH, START TO SHAKE, BITE YOUR LIP, HUFF AND PUFF, CROSS YOUR ARMS, THINK MEAN THOUGHTS, SHED A TEAR, HIT A PILLOW, RAISE YOUR VOICE."

Doesn't it sound **silly**
to sing about anger?

That's because we often think happiness is an emotion we want to encourage, and anger is one we want to avoid.

And there are lots
of reasons for that.

Maybe it's too scary
to talk about anger.

Maybe you feel too angry
to talk about your anger.

Or maybe, you don't know
how to bring up your anger.

That's **OK.**

That's why I'm sharing this story.

See, when I was in middle school,
I was bullied.

Being bullied every day made me
very angry.

Little by little,
I allowed my anger
to bottle up inside me.

I started making decisions
that hurt me and pushed away
the people I cared about.

That's because I didn't talk about
my anger or understand it.

It took me a long time to learn how to not let my anger control me and understand that feeling anger can actually be a good thing.

But once I did, it changed my life for the better.

I want to help you do the same.

So...what is **anger?**

Anger is an emotion that they've been hurt by

comes up when people feel
a person or situation.

Like when you're left out
or excluded from something.

When someone takes something
from you without asking.

When someone is mean to you and you don't know why.

Or when you're frustrated, or something doesn't go your way.

Anger is such a powerful emotion that we sometimes use it as a shield to protect us from the things that hurt or that we don't understand.

Anger is that **BIG.**

ANGER IS ALSO A

REAC

TO A MOMENT OR SITUATION THAT

TION

IS UNFAIR OR OUT OF YOUR CONTROL.

It's actually healthy to feel
angry once in a while!

Because it can help us
to let all those **BIG** feelings out.

But when we don't talk about our anger, it just keeps building and building until it becomes.........................

UNCONTR

OLLABLE.

When your anger
becomes uncontrollable,
it can make you do or say
things you will regret later.

It can even lead you to hurting yourself or others, which is why it's important not to let your emotions control you.

You may be asking,

"How can I control my anger?"

I know, I know.

Controlling your anger
might sound like
an impossible thing.

Because when you're angry you might feel like you're out of control.

You might feel really hot and your hands may begin to shake.

Sometimes your anger might even make you feel sick.

But I promise it's possible to control!

And I'm going to help you figure it out because I've been there.

So I want you to try something with me.

The next time you feel angry or out of control...

PAUSE

AND GIVE YOURSELF SPACE.

That could look like...

Taking some slow,
deep breaths, in and out.

Finding some quiet
time for yourself.

Watching your
favorite show.

Drawing a picture that
represents what you're feeling.

Or counting how many times
you can say Mississippi!

NOTICE

HOW YOU ARE FEELING AND NAME IT.

So—you're probably angry,
but are you also feeling...

Sad? Frustrated? Annoyed?
Jealous? Fearful? Anxious?
Scared? Disappointed?
Confused?

Does your head hurt?
Are you hungry? Are you tired?

Naming your anger's
partners will help.

THINK

ABOUT WHY YOU ARE FEELING THIS WAY.

Sometimes we don't know
why we're feeling angry,
so try to think back.

Did something happen?
Did someone say something?
Did someone not say something?

You can't always
do something about it
or find the cause,
but understanding why
you're feeling this way can
help you start to process*
your anger and let it go.

*To process something means to understand what happened,
what you're feeling, and why you might be feeling it.

ASK YOURSELF,

WHAT CAN I DO WITH THIS FEELING?

Once you've discovered
what hurts you and name it,
you can do something about it
because it's real.

What to do isn't always
simple or clear, and you can't
always get away from the things
that make you angry, but that
doesn't mean you have to
hold on to your anger.

You can find a way to...

LET IT OUT!

The key to letting it out is to first find a safe person you can trust.

Maybe that's your grownup, or your best friend, or your sibling, or your school counselor.

Then find a way to let them know how you feel.

Maybe that's just saying,

"I feel angry."

Or you could draw them a picture.

Or explain it with colors
or numbers instead of words.

Whatever feels right to you
and makes the most sense.

Wanna know something cool?

If you go through the steps...

you are practicing how to manage your thoughts and feelings.

Because it isn't about control—it's about managing your anger, which is super healthy.

And when you learn how
to manage your anger,
you can harness it
and use it for good!

IT'S TRUE!

Anger can be healthy.

And sometimes,
anger can work like fuel.

Because when we see or experience something that's unfair and we get angry, it can inspire us to help make positive change.

Whether that's in your family, school, or community.

It's up to you.

Like when you know someone
at your school is being bullied.

That might make you feel
really angry and maybe
a little sad or scared.

Well, you could use that anger to tell a grownup about what's going on so they can help.

That way, you can help people and make your school feel like a safer place.

I wish I could say that one day you won't feel any anger at all —but you will.

It's part of life
and that's **OK.**

Because now you know
what to do with it.

You can get angry,
and still be OK.

And your anger might be...

THE SPARK THAT LEADS TO POSITIVE CHANGE.

Outro

Can you see how anger can be a productive motivator? The more we talk about anger openly, the more we can understand how to manage it for our good and the good of others.

I was bullied in middle school and I bottled up my anger in an unhealthy way. To make matters worse, I didn't allow my anger to bring about change. Today, I help others understand why some people bully others and how we can all do our part in creating a stable learning environment for students.

Encourage your kids to talk about their anger and create a safe space for them to vent and process their emotions. Then, share a story about how you were able to use anger as a positive motivator. Whether that was in big ways like starting a business, or in small ways like starting a conversation.

If the world around us doesn't benefit from our anger—let it go.

About The Author

As a motivational speaker, Fabian Ramirez teaches audiences how to vent emotions in healthy ways. His passion for helping kids led him to write this book about a huge emotion we all experience: anger.

Growing up, Fabian was called "Biscuit" and was bullied because of his weight. He later became prom king of his high school and now, every audience he speaks to yells with excitement, "Run, Biscuit!" Fabian learned to turn something that made him angry into something positive.

Fabian wants readers to understand that they get to decide what to do with anger each time they feel it.

 @debtfreehispanic   /runbiscuit   🌐 FabianRamirez.com

a kids book about MONEY
by ...tramwasser

a kids book about BEING INCLUSIVE
by Ashton Mota & Rebekah Bruesehoff
in partnership with The GenderCool Project

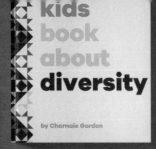
a kids book about diversity
by Charnaie Gordon

a kids book about LEADeRSHIP
by Orion Jean

a kids book about IMMIG...
by MJ Calder

a kids book about SAFETY
by Soraya Sutherlin, CEM
in partnership with JUDY

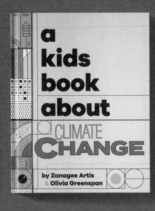
a kids book about CLIMATE CHANGE
by Zanagee Artis & Olivia Greenspan

a kids book about IMAGINATION
by LEVAR BURTON

a kids book about CONFIDENCE
by Joy Cho

a kids b... about S...
by ...

a kids book about ANXIETY
...abo ...Happy Faces

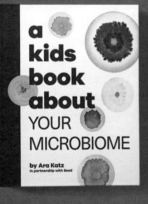
a kids book about YOUR MICROBIOME
by Ara Katz
in partnership with Seed

a kids book about racism
by Jelani Memory

a kids book about DISABILITIES
by Kristine Napper

a kids book abo bor
by: KyLe S...

a kids book about DIVORCE
by Ashley Simpo

a kids book about cancer
by Dr. Kelsie Storm & Sarah Porter

a kids book about BEING TRANSGENDER
by Gia Parr
in partnership with The GenderCool Project

a kids book about DEPRESSION
by Kileah McIlvain

a kids b... about ...
by ...

a kids book about ...ame

a kids book about THE TULSA RACE MASSACRE